Y0-CBP-089

Quelle Histoire
E D I T I O N S

Graphics: Quelle Histoire
Illustrations: Bruno Wennagel, Mathieu Ferret
Text: Albin Quéru et Romain Jubert

15 avenue de Villiers, 75017 Paris
© Quelle Histoire, Paris, 2014
Printed in France by Stin Imprimerie - Toulouse
Made by Labelfab www.labelfab.fr

Da Vinci

A Lonely Child

Leonardo was born on April 14, in 1452, in the town of Vinci in Italy, close to Florence, known at the time as the city of the arts. It is from this town that the child got his name – a name which would one day become famous! His father was a notary and his mother a peasant. Leonardo was separated from his mother at an early age and was raised by his father and his stepmother. What Leonardo loved more than anything was to walk alone and explore the Tuscan countryside. All things natural were of interest to him. For days on end he would observe and draw flowers, trees, clouds and animals.

———

1457

Verrocchio's Studio

In 1467, Leonardo's father relocated and took the boy to Florence with him. He showed his son's drawings to Master Verrocchio, a painter and a sculptor. The master took him on as an apprentice in his studio. Leonardo very quickly stood out because he painted shadow and light with considerable talent. So Verrocchio asked him to help him paint «The Baptism of Christ». Leonardo's task was to draw an angel. His figure was so beautiful that everyone's eyes are drawn to it when they look at the painting! According to legend, when Verrocchio first saw his student's work, filled with admiration, he broke his brush and gave up painting.

———

1469

The First Masterpieces

Leonardo constantly improved his painting techniques. He perfected an extraordinary process called «Sfumato». The figures are drawn without lines or borders and appear smoky. To paint successfully using this technique, several dozen very light coats of paint have to be superimposed upon each another. Each painting required months and months of work. Obviously Leonardo was late with his orders. Some were even cancelled. But he was looking for perfection and he got it!

1474

Milan

At this point Leonardo was known throughout Italy. In 1482, he left for Milan to enter into the service of the Duke of Sforza. The latter would commission him with largest horse statue in the world! Leonardo worked for 10 years on the sketches and the preliminary sculptures in order to create this 7-metre-high work in bronze. But the French soldiers of King Louis XII invaded Italy and the duke gave the 100 tons of bronze that were to be used to cast the statue to his army. Fortunately Leonardo had a number of other projects: he painted, became an architectural advisor and studied mechanics..

1482

In the Service of Cesare Borgia

Leonardo had to leave Milan, which had been taken by the French king, Louis XII. He entered into the service of the very wealthy Cesare Borgia as chief engineer. Cesare was a warrior and Leonardo followed him on his military campaigns. He presented him with extraordinary inventions to win his battles: an armoured tank, a submarine and even a machine gun! But at the time a motor to make them work did not exist and the inventions of our Leonardo were thought to be eccentric.

——

1502

Louis XII

The French, who greatly admired Leonardo, proposed that he work for them. Leonardo was delighted and returned to Milan where he entered into the service of the Duke of Amboise. For the visit of the king of France to Italy, Leonardo invented an incredible robot: a walking lion! The king asked Leonardo to become his military engineer. Leonardo accepted and began to work for Louis XII. He drew, notably, splendid maps with a 3D aspect. This was a great achievement.

1506

Tough Competition

In 1512, the French were defeated and left Italy. Leonardo then moved to Rome, but he was no longer the only famous Italian. New artists had come into vogue like Raphael and Michelangelo. Ever fewer people turned to him to build fortresses or to beautify the capital city. And the Pope chose Raphael to paint the dome of Saint Peter's Basilica in Rome! Disappointed, Leonardo left Italy for France.

1512

At the Court of the King of France

The new king of France, Francis I, was a great admirer of Leonardo. He named him «The First Painter, Architect and Mechanic of the King» and provided him with enormous resources so that Leonardo could create in total freedom. He even offered him the use of a manor, the Clos Lucé, near the castle of Amboise. Over 60 years old at the time, Leonardo spent many happy days organising parties and undertaking scientific research. Painting had become much more difficult as his right arm had become paralyzed. But it didn't matter: he finished his paintings with his left arm.

1516

The Legacy

Although he was very sick, Leonardo da Vinci continued to work on many projects. Francis I asked him to think up some plans for a new capital of France – Romorantin – and to build a palace there! Leonardo would not finish this work. He died at the Clos Lucé at the age of 67. According to his last wishes, he was buried in the chapel of the castle of Amboise and sixty beggars followed his cortege. He bequeathed his books and some of his works to his faithful student: Francesco Melzi.

———

1519

An Eternal Artist

Today when Leonardo da Vinci is talked about, it is as the «Genius of the Renaissance». A painter, architect, sculptor, engineer, scholar...he knew how to do all things – and did them all well! Numerous exhibitions display his paintings or sketches of his incredible inventions. But his best-known work remains the Mona Lisa. The painting of this unknown individual with a mysterious smile is the most visited work of art in the world.

2014

1450

1452
Birth of
Da Vinci

1469
Starts at
Verrocchio's
studio

1478
First
commissioned
paintings

1483
Da Vinci paints
«The Virgin of
the Rocks»

1467
Arrival in
Florence

1473
Leonardo's
first dated
picture

1482
Leonardo
leaves Florence
for Milan

1495
Sforza
commissions
«The Last Supper»

1499
The French take Milan

1502
Da Vinci enters the service of Cesare Borgia

1504
Leonardo's father dies

1515
Battle of Marignan

1519
Da Vinci dies

1500
Da Vinci returns to Florence

1503
Da Vinci paints «The Mona Lisa»

1512
Da Vinci enters the service of the Pope

1516
Francis I invites Da Vinci to France

1520

Europe in the 15th century

Key to the

MAP

1 Da Vinci's village

It is in this small village in Tuscany that Leonardo was born, and it is from here that he got his name: Da Vinci! As a child, Leonardo draws images from the natural world.

2 Florentine Renaissance

In the 15th century, the city of Florence was the art capital of Europe. Thanks to the rich Medici family, it attracted the greatest artists of the time.

3 The siege of Pisa

In 1503, Leonardo Da Vinci accompanied Cesare Borgia in the siege of Pisa. This is where he revealed his famous plans for tanks and machines of war.

4 The Duchy of Milan

After agreeing to enter the service of the Duke of Sforza, Da Vinci moved to Milan. He remained there for many years and produced several masterpieces.

5 Francis I and the arts

On becoming King of France, Francis I also became the first champion of the arts and of literature. During his reign, he brought many artists to his court.

6 The Clos Lucé

Francis I offered the use of this beautiful chateau in the heart of the city of Amboise in the Loire Valley to Leonardo Da Vinci as a sign of friendship.

Kingdom of France

Independent states

Spanish possessions

Holy Roman Empire

Kingdom of England

Portraits

Botticelli
(1444-1510)
The Florence-born Botticelli greatly impressed with his painting from a very young age. His style, which used contour lines, gave his paintings a great deal of originality. Da Vinci felt much admiration for him.

Verrocchio
(1435-1488)
The grand master of Florentine painting, he trained many artists such as Botticini, Perugino and Credi. But his most famous pupil remains Leonardo Da Vinci, who entered his service in 1469.

Raphael
(1483-1520)
A gifted painter, Raphael became
famous whilst still very young.
He admired Leonardo's style and
even visited his studio. Unfortunately,
he fell ill and died at just 37 years
of age.

Michelangelo
(1475-1564)
Vain and irascible, Michelangelo
drew scorn from other artists of
his time. Despite his personality, his
talent means that his is considered
one of the greatest geniuses
of the Renaissance.

IMAGE HUNT

Hunt for these pictures in the scene on the right:

Da Vinci

The gardener 1

The musician

The roofer

The black greyhound

Botticelli

The cook

The apprentice

The red greyhound

The thief

Francis I

The runaway

Verrocchio

Raphael

The gardener 2

The gardener 3

The sculptor

The grey greyhound

The workman

Michelangelo

Find the 7 differences between the left-hand and right-hand pictures

MAZE

Help Leonardo find his brushes...

SILHOUETTES

Which one is Leonardo Da Vinci's silhouette?

a.

b.

c.

d.

e.

Game

QUIZ

1. What was Da Vinci's first name?

    a. Lorenzo   b. Andrea

    c. Claudio   d. Leonardo

2. Which king offered Da Vinci Clos Lucé?

    a. Francis I   b. Louis XII

    c. Henry IV   d. Philip Augustus

3. Who was Da Vinci's favourite student?

    a. Michelangelo   b. Melzi

    c. Raphael   d. Botticelli

Correct answers: 1.d / 2.a / 3.b

Children's History collection
for an enjoyable learning experience!

Vercingetorix

Joan of Arc

Francis I of France

Louis XIV

Marie-Antoinette

Napoleon

Discover
the Quelle Histoire apps, too!

**A collection of interactive applications
to learn about history in a fun way!**

-2000	-1000	0	1000	200(

1452 - 1519

Quelle Histoire
EDITIONS

ISBN 978-2-37104-001

5 €

9782371040011